D1318985

# PLAYOFF PRESSURE

Renardo Barden

BASKETBALL HEROES

The Rourke Corporation, Inc.
Vero Beach, Florida 32964

Valley Park High School Library

Copyright 1992 by The Rourke Corporation, Inc.

All rights reserved. No part of this book may be reproduced or utilized in any form or by any means, electronic or mechanical, including photocopying, recording or by any information storage and retrieval system without permission in writing from the publisher.

The Rourke Corporation, Inc.
P.O. Box 3328, Vero Beach, FL 32964

Barden, Renardo.
  Playoff Pressure / by Renardo Barden.
    p.    cm. — (Basketball heroes)
  Includes bibliographical references and index.
  Summary: Examines significant moments in championship basketball playoffs of the past and discusses the psychological stresses they involved.
    ISBN 0-86593-162-3
    1. National Basketball Association—Juvenile literature. 2. Basketball—Tournaments—United States—Juvenile literature. 3. Basketball—United States—Psychological aspects—Juvenile literature. [1. Basketball—History.   2. Basketball—Psychological aspects.]
    I. Title.
  GV885.59.N37837    1992
  796.323'64'0973—dc20                                    92--9143
                                                          CIP
                                                          AC

Series Editor: Gregory Lee
Editor: Marguerite Aronowitz
Book design and production: The Creative Spark, San Clemente, CA
Cover photograph: D. Strohmeyer/ALLSPORT

Valley Park High School Library

# Contents

*The best players in basketball, such as Michael Jordan, are at their best when the pressure to win is greatest.*

# What Is Pressure?

**W**hen writing an account of a basketball game, a sportswriter might report that a player went "10 for 20." This means the player made ten of 20 attempted field goals. But no statistic can measure the pressure he experienced when scoring those points. Pressure—the tension or stress that can make or break a player's ability to compete—can be anything that happens on the basketball court, football field, or baseball diamond that can't be described by statistics.

During the National Basketball Association's 1991 Eastern Division playoffs, the Detroit Pistons tried to stop Michael Jordan from scoring by *double-teaming* him—surrounding him with two players every time he got the ball. This kind of competitive pressure can be seen. It's visible.

During the 1991 Western Division playoffs, Portland Trail Blazers' guard Terry Porter missed a last-second jump shot in the sixth and deciding game against the L.A. Lakers. It might have tied the score and taken the Blazers into a seventh game, but the shot missed and Portland's season was over. Many said Porter had "choked," or lost his control under pressure. When fans say this, they are talking about pressure that can't be seen, or mental pressure.

If asked, Porter might have said he didn't feel any pressure at all. He might have offered another reason for missing the shot. But during a playoff series, the pressure in professional sports is at its peak.

Many, many pressures, both visible and invisible, follow basketball players wherever they go. Players don't always acknowledge the pressure. Fans and sportswriters are free to guess that this or that event happened due to pressure.

Those of us who aren't professional athletes experience pressure at school, on the job, even at home. Sometimes pressure brings out our best—sometimes our worst. To feel pressure is to be human. To perform well under pressure can sometimes be heroic.

This book is about playoff pressure: the hundreds of big and little things that separate good players from great ones, strong teams from weak teams.

## Jordan Versus The Celtics

Sometimes pressure comes from expectations. This means what players, coaches, and fans *think* should be the result of any given matchup. A winning tradition can put a lot of pressure on the players who inherit that tradition.

In 1986, for example, the Boston Celtics were under playoff pressures the Chicago Bulls had yet to experience. Boston has a basketball tradition because the Celtics have won more world championships than any other team in the NBA. For many Boston fans it wasn't enough that their 1986 team had posted the season's best record; what they wanted was another *dynasty* (a team that wins consistently year after year).

Led by the great Bill Russell, Boston had been untouchable during the 1960s. In Russell's 13 years as a Celtic, the Boston dynasty won 11 world championships! No team had accomplished that before, and no team has done it since. So in 1986, with players like Larry Bird and Danny Ainge and Robert Parish, Celtics fans were

*Was it playoff pressure that made Portland's Terry Porter miss a crucial jump shot?*

already dreaming of another dynasty. If there is one truth about playoff pressure, it is this: The more a team wins, the more its fans come to expect victory.

In 1986, the Bulls didn't have to worry about the fans' hopes. They believed their new star, Michael Jordan, would someday lead the Bulls to a championship. But everybody—or at least everybody but Jordan—seemed to accept the talk going around that the Bulls weren't yet ready for a championship.

## A Record-Setting Sunday

During the first round of the 1986 Eastern Conference playoffs, Jordan had not yet established himself as one of the best players of all time. A broken foot had kept him out of most of the regular season. From the opening tip-off, however, the Celtics were frustrated trying to stop him.

When the final buzzer sounded that first Sunday in April of 1986, Jordan had scored 63 points—an amazing performance. Nobody had ever scored 63 points in a playoff game before. For Boston, Larry Bird had a game that was nearly as remarkable, putting up 36 points. And when he wasn't shooting, he was hopping from spot to spot, making things happen. By game's end he had nabbed twelve rebounds and eight assists.

With only a few seconds left in the second overtime, a tired Jordan missed a 12-foot jump shot and a chance to tie the game. The Celtics' Robert Parish snared the rebound and fed Bird, who dribbled down the right side of the court. As he pulled up to fire off one of his trademark jumpers, however, two Bulls—including the man guarding Parish—moved in to block the shot. At the last instant, Bird's shot became a pass to a wide-open Parish, who scored

*Larry Bird knows all about big game pressure—he won three MVP awards to prove it.*

with ease just before the buzzer sounded. The Celtics won the game 135-131.

Boston went on to sweep the series. A few weeks later, they had sewn up the world championship.

Under playoff conditions, basketball always seems to come down to this: no one player is good enough to carry a whole team. Without a balanced defense and offense, without ball sharing, without team play, a team can't win a game, much less a world championship.

Boston already knew this fact, but the Bulls had to learn it the hard way before they would become champions. And nobody knew this better than the L.A. Lakers.

In the final years of the 1960s, the Lakers fielded a team that included three of the top scorers in NBA history: Wilt Chamberlain, Elgin Baylor, and Jerry West. Never before and certainly not since has there been a team with such firepower. But the defense-minded Celtics, led by the shot-blocking Bill Russell and superb ball handlers such as Bob Cousy, K.C. Jones, and others, sent the Lakers home year after year without a trophy. Individual greatness was not enough in 1986 when the Bulls lost to the Celtics, and it wasn't enough in the days of Chamberlain and West.

During his 14-year career, Wilt Chamberlain played on only two championship teams: the 1966-67 Philadelphia 76ers and the 1971-72 Lakers. When the 76ers won, it was the first year in seven that Chamberlain did not win the NBA scoring title. And he was a non-factor in the twilight of his career when the Lakers won in 1972.

The big scoring and rebounding numbers Chamberlain posted early in his career never earned him a championship ring. In fact, until Michael Jordan's 1991 season, only one player had ever been the league's top scorer while playing on a world championship team: Kareem Abdul-Jabbar in 1971.

*Some fans said Scottie Pippen couldn't handle the pressure during the 1990 NBA semi-finals. But he proved them wrong during Chicago's 1991 championship victory.*

## The Mysterious Migraine

Sometimes pressure can be painful. In 1990, Chicago Bulls' forward Scottie Pippen came down with a migraine headache before Game 7 of the Eastern Conference finals against Detroit. Because of his headache, Pippen decided he was unable to play and took himself out of the game. When the Bulls lost, many people blamed Pippen. For the fans, it was another disappointing end to yet another playoff series. The Bulls had come close to winning several years running, but always choked, even with Michael Jordan.

Migraines are not imaginary, but there is medical evidence that they can be brought on by stress. Coming at the most crucial point in the Bulls' season, Pippen's headache might have been a sign of playoff pressure.

Following the finals, many NBA fans said Pippen lacked the qualities of a great player. They blamed him for not playing in spite of the pain, and he had to live with fan criticism for an entire year. Until he could prove he was not afraid of playoff pressure, Pippen would remain a *scapegoat*—someone who is blamed for the failure of many. As he later admitted, the memory of that famous headache became its own form of pressure during the 1991 finals when the Bulls got another chance against the Pistons. And so did Pippen.

The Pistons fell quickly. Then Pippen responded against the Lakers in the finals by logging more game minutes than any other Bull. Finishing with a flourish, he racked up a scoring average of more than 20 points and nine rebounds per game. During the final game Pippen poured in 32 points.

Had Pippen's migraine been a response to playoff pressure? One fan said that perhaps Pippen had proved headaches were contagious: He'd just given a big one to the Pistons.

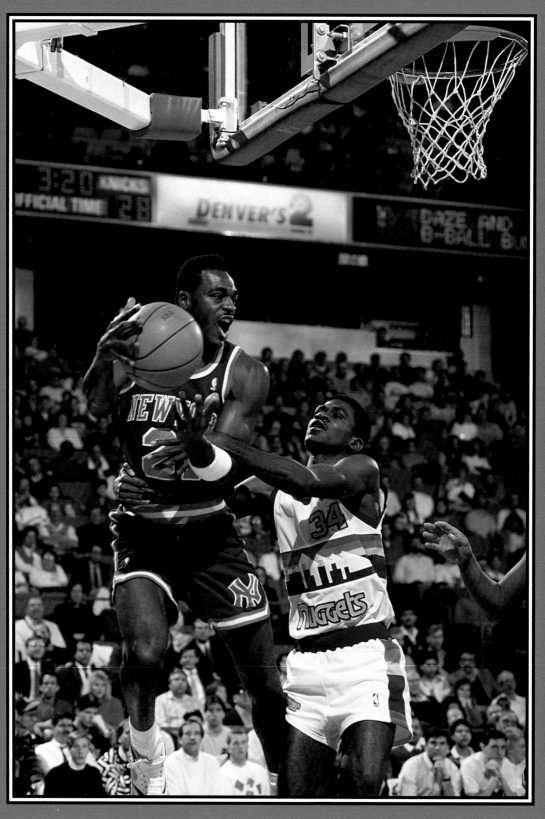

*Teams battle for more than 80 games during the regular NBA season
before facing each other in a grueling series of playoff rounds.*

# The Long Season

**U**nder the current playoff system, each April the 16 most successful of the NBA's 27 teams are admitted to the playoffs. It takes three rounds of best-of-five and best-of-seven games to reduce the field to the two conference winners. The teams that emerge from this large pack meet in a best-of-seven-game championship series in June.

Some fans feel that a six-week playoff series that allows more than half of the league's teams a chance to win the championship doesn't need a regular season of 82 games. When more than half of the teams are eligible, the regular season standings seem unimportant.

For example, when the Chicago Bulls made it to the 1986 playoffs, they had

### Basketball Trivia

**Q:** *What was the longest game in the history of the National Basketball Association?*
**A:** *On January 6, 1951, the Rochester Royals met the Indianapolis Olympians in a game that ran through six overtime periods and lasted a total of 78 minutes.*

**Q:** *Who was the first professional basketball player to be sold to another team?*
**A:** *In 1917 Clarence Johnson was sold by his team, the Baslos Globetrotters, to another team in Fond du Lac, Wisconsin.*

a record of 30-52. Why should a team with so poor a record play in the championships? Surely the fact that the Celtics had won twice as many regular season games as the Bulls proved that Boston was the better team. The point is, a decent team is not under a lot of "must win" pressure during the long regular season, but pressure surfaces in other ways.

First, there is the home court advantage. Teams definitely win at home much more than they win on the road. When the NBA schedules more playoff games in a team's home city, it usually means a better win-loss record.

## Injuries

Since 1984, when the present playoff structure was adopted, any NBA team winning half its regular season makes it into the playoffs. In effect, once a team wins approximately 41 games, it can keep its best players off the floor for the rest of the season. A team's stars can recover from pain and fatigue on the bench and avoid injuries that might keep them out of the playoffs.

In the 1991 playoffs, one of the many advantages the Bulls had was their lack of injuries. The Detroit Pistons weren't so lucky. Guard Isiah Thomas had missed 34 regular season games with an injured wrist, and his teammate Joe Dumars was hobbled by an injured toe. The Lakers were also weak going into the finals, as James Worthy and Byron Scott were both ailing.

The Bulls were quick to capitalize on their strength, first by eliminating their pesky Eastern Conference rivals. The Pistons, back-to-back NBA champions, were swept in four games. Then, knowing that the Lakers' top scorers were limited on offense, the Bulls swarmed all over Magic Johnson, limiting his scoring.

*Two Hall of Famers in their prime: Sam Jones (right) of Boston takes on Oscar Robertson.*

At the end of the second quarter in Game 4, the Bulls pulled away from the Lakers for good. Worthy reinjured his ankle, and Scott hurt his shoulder. The Lakers had to rely on newcomers having little playoff experience. The Bulls took just five games to wrap up the championship.

## Fatigue

Weary players can be a team's downfall in playoff games. Playoff success often goes to the team that is most rested. The physical and emotional stress of running up and down the court begins to affect play long before the end of the 82-game regular season.

Hall of Famer Walt Frazier recalled a tough stretch during the 1969-70 season, the year the New York Knicks won the world championship:

"We beat Detroit in the Garden by one point Christmas night, then caught a midnight flight to Los Angeles. We arrived at L.A. International at 3:30 a.m. [6:30 a.m. New York time]. We lost by 12 points that night at the Forum. We were up at 6:45 the next morning for a flight to Vancouver that arrived at 11:15 a.m. That night we beat Seattle by two. We were roused [sic] out of bed at 5:45 a.m. for a six-hour, three-stop flight to Phoenix and beat the Suns that night by nineteen. How, I don't know. We flew home, finishing off a trip of more than 7,000 miles. We changed our name from the Knicks to the Zombies."

Fatigue is a definite playoff pressure, and often a team's opponents use it as a weapon. According to Hall of Famer Dolph Schayes (whose son Danny now plays for the Milwaukee Bucks), former Boston Celtics' coach Red Auerbach was a master at exploiting fatigue. One of Auerbach's favorite ploys was to tire an opposing team's best shooter by forcing him to play rough defense.

"Red realized you could nullify a player's offensive output a bit if you made him work harder at the other end of the court," Schayes said.

Exhaustion was certainly a factor in the 1991 playoffs. While Chicago breezed past the Knicks by winning three straight, the Pistons struggled with Atlanta. Next, while the Bulls crushed Philadelphia in five, the Celtics put the Pistons through a six-game war. So when the Bulls and Pistons met in the semifinals, the Bulls were the fresher team. The Pistons were exhausted, and they played like it.

## Rough Stuff

Before becoming a superstar, Larry Bird played college basketball at Indiana State University. Once before an important game, fans asked him if it was as rough under the backboards as it looked. Without a word, Bird lifted his shirt and revealed ugly purple bruises on his chest.

George Mikan, the first great center in pro basketball, lost four front teeth in his first game as a Minneapolis Laker. Mikan's Hall of Fame career also included a broken leg, a broken nose, two broken foot bones, four broken fingers, and cuts that required 166 stitches.

Although he avoided plenty of contact (and almost never fouled out of a game), Wilt Chamberlain was often the target of rough play. Even though few opponents would have dared cross him off the court, on the floor Chamberlain was abused by opponents who tried to limit his scoring and rebounding.

Rough basketball is discouraged by the NBA, but has recently come back into fashion thanks to teams such as the Detroit Pistons. At six-feet, eight-inches, and 250 pounds, Rick Mahorn was one of the originators of the bruising style of defense played by today's Pistons. In fact, Mahorn paid out $11,000 in fines in 1988 for his physical aggressiveness on the court. When he dealt Utah Jazz center Mark Price a brain concussion, he was fined $5,000. Many thought he should have been suspended as well. During that same year, Mahorn mixed it up with Houston's Hakeem Olajuwon, Cleveland's Larry Nance, and most of the Chicago Bulls.

Bill Laimbeer also carries on this tradition. The 1988 season cost Pistons' players big bucks. Laimbeer had to shell out $6,000 for his own banging style of play. But bruising basketball can be as damaging to the team dishing it out as it is to the opponents. Winners of world

*Bill Laimbeer of the Detroit Pistons is known for giving opponents a hard time under the basket.*

championships in 1989 and 1990, the Pistons might well have won it all in 1988 too, if it weren't for late season injuries to Isiah Thomas and Rick Mahorn.

## The Playoffs

Many fans want a simpler, shorter playoff system similar to pro baseball. After 82 games, the regular season has—for the most part—already identified the best teams. In fact, since 1979, nearly all the NBA finals champions have been the teams with the best regular season records. So what is the point of holding playoffs that give most teams in the NBA a chance—even a small chance—to undo the regular season's results?

One opinion is that the playoffs allow for the chance of an upset. They give so-called "underdogs" a second chance to prove themselves under playoff pressure. Fans like a team capable of playing brilliantly under pressure, and just such a team emerged in 1977.

## The Comeback Series

In the middle 1970s, the Portland Trail Blazers acquired a big center named Bill Walton. Like Kareem Abdul-Jabbar, Walton had been a star with John Wooden's UCLA Bruins. With the Blazers, however, Walton became injury-prone. When he was healthy, he was very good. But there were too many games when he couldn't play.

At the beginning of the 1976 season, the Blazers' prospects didn't look good. Despite Walton's obvious talents, Portland was still a fairly new club that had never made the playoffs. In their first seven years in the NBA, they had never won even 50 percent of their games.

But in 1977, Portland played better than ever. They finished with a 49-33 record. That was third-best in the Western Conference, and the second-best record

*Bill Walton's rebounding helped make the difference in Portland's amazing come-from-behind win during the NBA finals in 1977.*

in their Pacific Division. It was good enough to get Portland into the playoffs.

To the surprise of nearly everyone, Portland got hot in the playoffs and defeated the Denver Nuggets. Then they bounced the Lakers out in four straight—and both Denver and L.A. had better regular season records.

Philadelphia, too, was on a roll. The 76ers stormed past Boston and Houston, with the brilliant Julius "Dr. J" Erving throwing down shot after shot. The 76ers went on to win the first two games of the NBA finals against Portland.

With Portland two games back, many Oregon fans braced for defeat. But the Blazers caught fire. Every missed shot seemed to turn into a Walton rebound. Jerry Lucas nailed everything he put up. Then, to the fans' amazement, the Blazers came from behind and won the next four games to become the NBA champions.

Portland's triumph went down in basketball history as "the Comeback Season." Underdogs everywhere grew hopeful. Not only did the team with the fourth-best regular season record win the championship, it did it so by coming back from a two-game deficit.

The following year, the Washington Bullets—a team with the third-best record in the East—met and defeated the Seattle Supersonics, a team with the fourth-best record in the West. This series provided more proof that playoff pressure could create exciting basketball.

Valley Park High School Library

*Wilt Chamberlain (13) was so dominating on the basketball court that several rules were permanently changed to give his opponents a fighting chance.*

# New Rules, More Pressure

**U**ntil recently, basketball teams often cared about just one thing: keeping possession of the ball no matter what. Players risked only the simplest shots. Basketball was a game of passing, attempted steals, and fouling. Televised games looked like a series of endless passes, followed by pauses at the free-throw line.

Today, the score of an NBA game can easily be 19-18 before a team calls its first time out. But on November 22, 1950, the Fort Wayne Pistons beat the Minneapolis Lakers with a final score of just 19-18. It wasn't because the Pistons and Lakers had bad shooting skills, as just 31 shots were taken during the entire game!

Less than two months later, the Rochester Royals met the Indianapolis Olympians in a game that dragged through six overtime periods. The Olympians won 75-73, but fewer than two points were scored for every minute of play. The game lasted a record-setting 78 minutes, with just 23 shots taken during the six overtime periods.

Many years later, on December 13, 1983, in a game that went into three overtimes, the Pistons defeated the Denver Nuggets by a score of 186-184. Obviously, something happened between 1950 and 1983 to encourage scoring. It was called the 24-second shot clock.

## The 24-Second Shot Clock

Many years ago, some smart people realized that television might make professional basketball a profitable business. They also knew that basketball would have to do its part by becoming more exciting. At a team owners' meeting in 1951, Milwaukee Hawks' coach Red Holzman proposed a rule that he hoped would make long, low-scoring games a thing of the past. Both Holzman and Syracuse Nationals' owner Danny Biasone wanted a rule that would force teams to attempt to score within 24 seconds of gaining possession.

With such a rule, teams would have to shoot, move the ball quickly from one side of the court to the other, and keep the game moving. The NBA adopted the 24-second shot clock rule, and the faster pace began making the game more exciting. Outlet passes, fast breaks, posting up, dribbling, running, and driving skills became more important. Foot speed and endurance meant more than strength. Shooting accuracy at a faster pace was essential. Throughout the entire league, team scoring jumped to an average of 93 points per team per game, an increase of almost 15 points.

Playoff pressure changed accordingly. The search for players who could drive, shoot, and rebound quickly was on. And the relentless clock, reset after each field goal, made players move up and down the court with few pauses.

## More Rule Changes

In 1959, a seven-foot, one-inch center shattered the all-time NBA scoring record. In his debut with the Philadelphia Warriors, rookie Wilt Chamberlain came into the league like a one-man revolution. Whether shooting or rebounding, Chamberlain was almost impossible to stop. He led the league in scoring seven times, scored 2,000 or more points in seven consecutive seasons, and led the league in rebounding 11 times.

In an effort to limit his impact on the game, the NBA made some rule changes. One rule reduced to three seconds the length of time a player could remain in the *free-throw lane*—the painted area under the basket. This meant a player couldn't just stand in the lane and wait for a good pass, he had to keep moving. Now that players had more to think about, game pressure increased.

Teams searched for other ways to stop Chamberlain. Because he was such a poor free-throw shooter, Chamberlain was often deliberately fouled. During the 1966-67 season, Chicago Bulls' coach Johnny Kerr was determined to hold down Chamberlain's scoring. He knew that Chamberlain shot only about 40 percent from the free-throw line, so he told his players to deliberately foul Chamberlain every time he got the ball. Kerr didn't care if his entire bench fouled out.

Chamberlain realized what was happening, and so did the NBA. Shortly afterwards, the league created another rule: Any team deliberately fouling another

*Sometimes the pressure makes players want to let it all out!*

*Tough defense can pressure the other team into making mistakes. Here, John Havlicek (left) guards a fellow Hall of Fame player, Walt Frazier.*

26

player would be given a *technical*. When a technical is called, the fouled team is allowed to send its best shooter to the line. After the free throw, the fouled team also gets possession of the ball. Understandably, this rule discouraged deliberate fouls.

By adopting rules that would make the game more exciting, the NBA was applying playoff pressure to both the teams and the players. The NBA was speeding up the game, penalizing rough play, and rewarding shooting. The teams responded by playing a different brand of basketball.

## Strategy Through Defense

By the end of a regular season, all teams know their own strengths and weaknesses—and those of their rivals. This familiarity makes strategy even more important.

Timeouts are used carefully. Game plans are changed from quarter to quarter. Players are sent in and pulled off the court according to a team's needs at the moment. Coaches talk intently with every player and assistant coach, and yell at the referees. Coaches try to create a strategy that will force the other team to make mistakes.

Going into the 1989 playoffs, the Golden State Warriors were 2-2 against the Utah Jazz during the regular season. The Jazz had won the Midwest Division, while the Warriors had barely qualified in the tough Pacific Division.

Golden State knew that to get past Utah they would have to stop power forward Karl Malone, who finished just behind Jordan in scoring that year. Malone was the "go-to" guy, averaging better than 29 points a game. The Warriors decided that the best way to stop Malone was to prevent the league's assist leader, John Stockton, from getting the ball to Malone.

*Bill Russell was hired by the Celtics for his great defense, and he helped bring more championships to Boston than any other single player.*

Their strategy was to let Stockton do anything he wanted except pass the ball to Malone. By keeping Malone covered, Golden State forced Stockton to do more shooting and try to make difficult shots. The Warriors took the Jazz in three straight games.

Sports fans believe in a popular theory: offensive skills may get a team into a championship, but defensive skills are what win it. Blocked shots, defensive rebounds, steals, and free throws can make the difference between losing and winning.

Whether this is true or not, defense does take on added importance during the playoffs. Since shooting baskets involves split-second timing and a delicate touch, the pressure generated in the playoffs often affects a team's shooting. Even the best offense usually falters a bit in the playoffs.

When Chuck Daly joined the Detroit Pistons as coach in 1983, Detroit had a reputation as a good shooting team. But there were other big shooting teams, too, and the Pistons were regularly outgunned by both the 76ers and the Celtics. Defensively, the Pistons ranked near the bottom in most categories.

Daly decided to put some balance in the team. He acquired physical players such as John Salley and Dennis Rodman. By the mid-1980s, the Pistons were a strong defensive team and making the playoffs.

In 1988-89, 16 teams outscored the Pistons, but they were second in overall defense and ended up becoming world champions. In 1989-90, 18 teams outscored the Pistons, but when the season was over the Pistons had held their opponents to under 100 points 13 times. Opponents going up against Rodman, Laimbeer, and company scored fewer than 45 percent of their shots from the floor. And once again Detroit won the world championship.

*One of the great matchups in NBA playoff history happened in 1983, and featured Kareem Abdul-Jabbar vs. Moses Malone.*

# Referees And Big Talk

**I**f Bill Laimbeer embodies the tough, defensive style of the Pistons, the Utah Jazz defense is represented by another, big center: Mark Eaton. Like Laimbeer, Eaton doesn't score much. Unlike Laimbeer, Eaton doesn't fight, foul out, or try to intimidate. He has never been fined for fighting, yet for years he has anchored one of the stingiest defensive teams in the league.

Tom Chambers had this to say of Eaton: "He's the only guy in the league that tries to guard the whole team and not just his man."

Eaton's seven-foot, four-inch frame—all 290 pounds of it—gives him an immediate advantage. Until Eaton came along, no NBA player had ever blocked 400 shots in a single season. In 1984-85,

---

**Basketball Trivia**

**Q:** Who was the greatest free throw shooter of all time?
**A:** Harold "Bunny" Levitt, who used to travel with the Harlem Globetrotters in the 1930s. He didn't play, he just went to the free-throw line. In one contest in 1935, Levitt sank 499 in a row before missing one. After nearly eight hours and 871 baskets, he had still missed only one.

**Q:** Who is the best free-throw shooter in the NBA today?
**A:** Veteran Moses Malone leads the NBA in free throws made with more than 8,000. Rick Barry had the best free-throw percentage of any player in history (.900).

Eaton batted away 456 shots and managed to block at least one shot per game in 94 consecutive games. In 1988, when Eaton led the league in blocked shots, the Jazz nearly knocked the Lakers out of the playoffs. Eaton still has a chance to break Abdul-Jabbar's career record of 3,189 blocked shots.

Shot blocking seems like a small part of the game, and it is. But like few other things in basketball, a blocked shot can hurt a good shooter's confidence. A good block can "psych out" a shooter and affect his accuracy for the rest of the game. Some pressures, in other words, are simply seeds of doubt planted in a player's mind. It is sometimes said that his "mental game" suffers.

One of the masters of the mental game was Boston Celtics' coach Red Auerbach.

## Referees

Back in the days when it was okay to smoke in public buildings, Auerbach sometimes lit a cigar toward the end of a game. Since it was known that he only lit a cigar to celebrate a significant Boston victory, opposing coaches and teams sometimes reacted to Auerbach's cigar. Angered by Auerbach's lighting up while the game was still in progress, opposing teams often made last-minute mistakes that ended up costing them the game.

Auerbach had other gimmicks. He made a point of arguing every close call with a referee. He didn't do this because he thought the referee was always wrong, he did it because he believed a referee would hesitate to make another call against the Celtics if he knew he would get yelled at.

"In our sport," Auerbach said, "the coach who takes a nap on the bench deserves to get the worst of the calls." Because they are not allowed on the floor, however, coaches are limited in the kind of pressure

*A successful drive-and-stuff can be a good intimidator, as former Lakers foward Elgin Baylor demonstrates.*

they can apply against other teams.

Players are not. Since officials have a tough job, players do what they can to take advantage of it. Dolph Schayes said that his reputation as a good offensive player earned him many advantages on the court.

"The guy with the reputation got the best calls," Schayes remembers. "I always had the best defensive man playing me, but after you get a reputation, you get what they call a license. Consequently, on any close call, the referees would give the offense the better part of it."

The originator of the "In Your Face Disgrace" slam dunk was the one and only Darryl Dawkins, who joined the Philadelphia 76ers in 1975. Dawkins drove into the lane like a runaway truck. Rough play and jive talk were Dawkins' specialties. He dubbed himself "the Duke of Intergalactic Dunkmanship." Dawkins' dunks were so strong that he broke more than one NBA backboard, raining broken glass onto the floor.

Dawkins never became a truly great player, but he knew how to worry his defenders. Would you want to guard a player who might pull the backboard down on top of you? Because of Dawkins, the NBA made safety-related changes to rims and backboards.

Of course a player doesn't have to demolish backboards to make an impression on his rivals. Athletes know that a few well-timed and well-chosen words can also affect an opponent's play.

## Big Talk

Going into the 1989 playoffs, the Bulls had to look at an unpleasant first series. During the regular season that year, the Cleveland Cavaliers had beaten Chicago six times. The Bulls had not managed to return the favor. While the Bulls struggled to keep a positive mental attitude, many Chicago fans despaired. How could the Bulls hope to win three games under playoff

*Magic Johnson always showed great confidence during the many playoff series he played.*

conditions against a team that had beaten them six times that season?

Michael Jordan predicted that the Bulls would beat the Cavs in four straight games. Whether or not he believed his own prediction, he did this partly for the benefit of the media. He knew his comments would be published and broadcasted. In fact, he figured that his comments would be posted in the Cavs' clubhouse. Jordan had another motive as well. He wanted to do something to inspire and motivate his teammates.

It is unlikely that Jordan's prediction worried the Cavaliers, but it is possible that his comments motivated his teammates. Chicago sportswriters doubted Jordan, but the Bulls responded by steaming past the Cavs 3-2. Then they trampled the hopes of the New York Knicks 4-2.

When they went on to win two games against the Pistons in the Eastern Conference finals, most people realized that Chicago was closer to a championship than ever before. But in the first game, the pressure was on as Jordan was double-teamed by Rodman and Dumars. And the Pistons played like thugs. Laimbeer was ejected from a game for elbowing after being involved in a scuffle with Scottie Pippen. Thomas was given a technical for mouthing off to a referee. And Rodman drew a technical of his own for deliberately head-butting the ball out of bounds.

In Game 2, however, Jordan let everyone know that he was not going to be intimidated by the Pistons' "bad boys" any more. Late in the first period, he stole the ball and drove for the basket. But instead of sprinting, he deliberately slowed down. Bill Laimbeer lumbered up behind him in the hope of blocking his shot, Jordan stuttered, then slam-dunked over the big Piston. As the ball went through the net, Jordan turned and glared defiantly at Laimbeer. The Pistons' pressure techniques had back fired.

In the 1980-81 finals, it was the Houston Rockets taking on the Boston Celtics for the championship. With the series tied at two games apiece, Moses Malone—normally a quiet man—told the press that the Celts weren't all that good. He even said that "with four guys off the street" from his hometown, he could beat the Celtics. The newspapers printed the comments, and Celtics' coach Bill Fitch pasted them to every locker in the Boston dressing room.

In Game 5, the Celtics blew the Rockets out of the water, 109-80. Cedric Maxwell, working against Malone, scored 24 points and took down 15 rebounds. In Game 6, Larry Bird emerged from a scoring slump to lead the Celts to the championship. Sometimes, as the saying goes, it is better to let "sleeping dogs lie." That means it is usually better to avoid getting your opponent angry. Strong play will beat strong words any day. But sometimes athletes who are under pressure, or who hear negative comments about themselves, just can't resist opening their mouths.

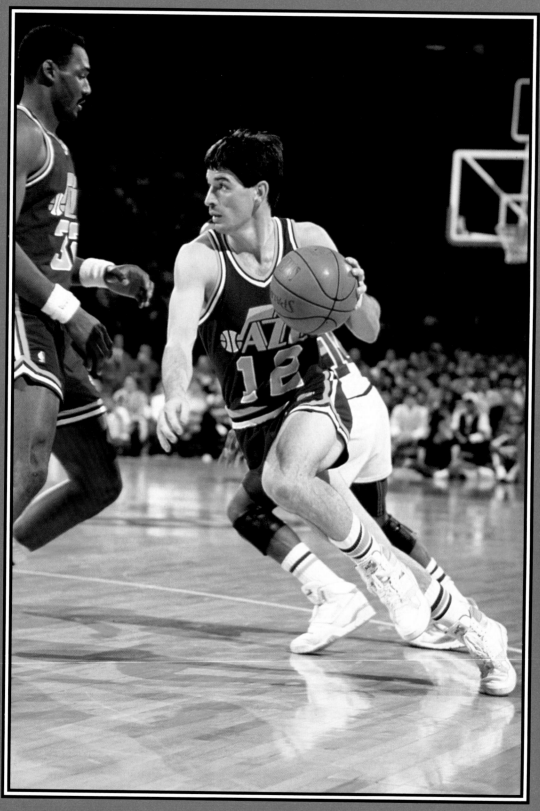

*John Stockton and the Utah Jazz have made the NBA playoffs several times, but never entered the NBA Finals.*

# Coaching Pressure

Other than the ball itself, one of the most movable aspects of basketball is the coach. In the NBA, coaches move a lot because they are hired and fired so often.

For example, in 1990 the New York Knicks fired coach Stu Jackson after just 15 regular season games. To replace him they brought in John MacLeod. One season later he was replaced by Pat Riley, the ex-Laker coach. Houston Rockets coach Don Chaney was fired in 1992 after the All-Star break, just a few months after being named Coach of the Year. And Chuck Daly, who coached Detroit to NBA titles in 1989 and 1990, was fired by Cleveland after coaching the Cavs for just 41 games in 1981-82.

Sometimes a coach's life comes down to a simple rule: win or be fired. Firing a coach may sometimes seem unfair, but players and team owners only look at one thing. It is the job of a coach to produce a winning team. Those who fail to do this—even if the players aren't that good—will be fired sooner or later.

An NBA player is expected to be able to dribble, pass, rebound, drive, shoot, defend, and sink free throws. But a good coach is expected to know more about basketball than his players. He must learn the strong point of each of his players, and train them to perform consistently. He has to deal with the media when his players are praised and criticized. He disputes foul calls, but must avoid getting a technical, or worse, being kicked out of a game. He must travel many thousands of miles a year. And, of course, he must get along with the owner or owners of the team who sign his paycheck.

Almost always, an NBA coach is faced with the difficult task of having to persuade pros to play the game his way. By the time NBA players reach the pros, they have already been coached by many different men. Knowing their own strengths and weaknesses, NBA players often resist change. So the pressure is on the coach to convince the team to play his way, and the fact that players often make a lot more money than coaches can make his job twice as hard.

## The Bull By The Horns

When Phil Jackson joined the Bulls in 1989 as the team's new coach, he knew he had talented players, including Mr. Talent himself, Michael Jordan. But he also could see that the Bulls had developed the habit of relying too much on Jordan. Other good players like Horace Grant, Bill Cartwright, and Scottie Pippen were reluctant to get in Jordan's way. Because of this, teams like Detroit were often able to double- and triple-team Michael and stop the Bulls cold. Jackson knew he had to get the players to divide up responsibilities.

During the 1990-91 season, Jordan agreed to share offensive duties and encourage his teammates. When the Bulls finally won the 1991 world championship, it was because Jordan had opened up his game and was doing more than shooting. In the finals, when the Lakers began to double- and even triple-team him, Jordan successfully passed to teammates Pippen, Grant, and John Paxson.

Game 2 was a classic contest. Grant and

Cartwright went on the offensive, and by themselves scored more than half the Bulls' first 30 points. Jordan passed to teammates and waited his chance.

Jackson gave the assignment of guarding Magic Johnson to Scottie Pippen. With the help of Cartwright and others, he used his quickness and long arms to contain the Lakers' key player. In this way, the Bulls were able to keep Jordan fresh.

Then, in the fourth quarter, Jordan exploded with a series of drives and jump shots. The Lakers couldn't keep up. The Bulls won by a convincing score of 107-86, helped by the 10-10 shooting of Paxson. The Bulls had shot 61.7 percent, an all-time high for a playoff game!

Phil Jackson had been the right man for the job. He had coped with the pressure of only his second season as an NBA coach, and brought the championship trophy home to Chicago.

**Riding Pressure To The Top**

Some basketball stars like Jordan, Malone, Charles Barkley, and Dominique Wilkins are great shooters. Others, like Hakeem Olajuwon, David

*Playing center for the New York Knicks is a high pressure job—ask Patrick Ewing.*

*Michael Jordan demonstrates one way of coping with playoff pressure.*

Robinson, or Dennis Rodman, are outstanding rebounders and shot blockers. Moses Malone, Larry Bird, and Portland's Buck Williams are deadly from the free-throw line. And others, like John Stockton or Isiah Thomas, know how to get the ball to an open man.

What separates the merely good NBA players from lasting basketball fame and fortune? Playoff success. For example, Alex English, Adrian Dantley, Walter Davis, and Jack Sikma are successful and established NBA players. Each has had a lengthy career and is among the leading scorers in NBA history. But their names are not as well known as they might be because they have not played on teams that handled pressure well.

In contrast, Larry Bird and Magic Johnson are joining the ranks of basketball's immortals because they responded well to playoff pressure. Basketball greats actually become better when the minutes tick by and the game is on the line. Just as the regular season leads to the playoffs, so the playoffs can lead to fame and fortune. And those players who use the pressure of competition to their advantage can earn themselves a place in history. In this sport, it will be a place in the Basketball Hall of Fame.

# Stats

| Top 20 NBA Coaches † | Yrs | W | L | Percentage |
|---|---|---|---|---|
| Red Auerbach | 20 | 99 | 69 | .589 |
| Jack Ramsay | 21 | 44 | 58 | .431 |
| Dick Motta | 21 | 56 | 70 | .444 |
| Bill Fitch | 20 | 54 | 48 | .529 |
| Gene Shue | 22 | 30 | 47 | .390 |
| Lenny Wilkens | 18 | 43 | 41 | .512 |
| Cotton Fitzsimmons | 18 | 30 | 42 | .417 |
| Red Holzman | 18 | 58 | 47 | .552 |
| John MacLeod | 18 | 47 | 54 | .465 |
| Don Nelson | 14 | 50 | 55 | .476 |
| Doug Moe | 14 | 33 | 50 | .398 |
| Pat Riley | 9 | 102 | 47 | .685 |
| Al Attles | 14 | 31 | 30 | .508 |
| K.C. Jones | 9 | 81 | 57 | .587 |
| Billy Cunningham | 8 | 66 | 39 | .629 |
| Alex Hannum | 12 | 45 | 34 | .570 |
| Chuck Daly | 9 | 69 | 39 | .639 |
| John Kundla | 11 | 60 | 35 | .632 |
| Tommy Heinsohn | 9 | 47 | 33 | .588 |
| Larry Costello | 10 | 37 | 23 | .617 |

† Playoff records through 1990-91 season

## All-Time Playoff Scoring Leaders †

|  | Yrs | Games | Pts | Avg |
|---|---|---|---|---|
| Kareem Abdul-Jabbar | 18 | 237 | 5762 | 24.3 |
| Jerry West | 13 | 153 | 4457 | 29.1 |
| Larry Bird | 11 | 160 | 3852 | 24.1 |
| John Havlicek | 13 | 172 | 3776 | 22.0 |
| Magic Johnson | 12 | 186 | 3640 | 19.6 |
| Elgin Baylor | 12 | 134 | 3623 | 27.0 |
| Wilt Chamberlain | 13 | 160 | 3607 | 22.5 |
| Dennis Johnson | 13 | 180 | 3116 | 17.3 |
| Julius Erving | 11 | 141 | 3088 | 21.9 |
| James Worthy | 8 | 138 | 2953 | 21.4 |
| Kevin McHale | 11 | 155 | 2941 | 19.0 |
| Sam Jones | 12 | 154 | 2909 | 18.9 |
| Bill Russell | 13 | 165 | 2673 | 16.2 |
| Robert Parish | 12 | 164 | 2616 | 16.0 |
| Michael Jordan | 7 | 70 | 2425 | 34.6 |
| Bob Pettit | 9 | 88 | 2240 | 25.5 |
| Elvin Hayes | 10 | 96 | 2194 | 22.9 |
| Isiah Thomas | 8 | 106 | 2191 | 20.7 |
| George Mikan | 9 | 91 | 2141 | 23.5 |
| Moses Malone | 12 | 94 | 2077 | 22.1 |

† Through 1991 playoffs

# Glossary

**CHOKE.** To lose control under pressure; to ruin a winning opportunity.

**DOUBLE TEAM.** When two players on the same team are assigned to cover and guard one player on the opposing team.

**DYNASTY.** A sports team that wins consistently year after year.

**FREE-THROW LANE.** The painted area or *key* just beneath and in front of the backboard on the court.

**HOME COURT ADVANTAGE.** In general, teams usually win more when they are playing in front of the home town fans.

**PRESSURE.** The tension and stress that can make or break a player's ability to compete.

**SCAPEGOAT.** An individual who takes the blame for a team loss.

**TECHNICAL.** A foul called for deliberately breaking certain rules.

**UNDERDOG.** The team or player who is not expected to win a competition.

# Bibliography

Aaseng, Nathan. *Basketball's High Flyers*. Minneapolis: Lerner Publications, 1980.

Abdul-Jabbar, Kareem with Mignon McCarthy. *Kareem*. New York: Random House, 1990.

Axthelm, Peter. *The City Game*. New York: A Harper's Magazine Press Book, 1970.

Bird, Larry with John Bischoff. *Bird On Basketball*. Reading, Massachusetts: Addison-Wesley, 1983.

Carter and Sachare. *The Sporting News Official NBA Guide, 1991-92*. St. Louis: Times-Mirror, 1991.

Fox, Larry. *The Illustrated History of Basketball*. Long Island City: Grosset & Dunlap, 1974.

Goldpaper and Pincus. *How To Talk Basketball*. New York: Dembner Books, 1983.

Holzman, Red and Harvey Frommer. *Red On Red*. New York: Bantam, 1987.

Jarrett, William S. *Timetables Of Sports History—Basketball*. New York: Facts on File, 1990.

Kerr, Johnny and Terry Pluto. *Bull Session*. Chicago: Bonus Books, 1989.

Salzberg, Charles. *From Set Shot to Slam Dunk*. New York: E.P. Dutton, 1987.

Shaughnessy, Dan. *Ever Green*. New York: St. Martin's Press, 1990.

Wolff, Alexander and Armen Keteyian. *Raw Recruits*. New York: Pocket Books, 1990.

## Photo Credits

ALLSPORT USA: 4, 25 (Stephen Dunn); 7, 41, 42 (Jim Gund); 8 (Damian Strohmeyer); 10, 12, 38 (Tim DeFrisco); 18, 35 (Mike Powell)

The Bettmann Archive: 15, 20, 33

Wide World Photos: 22, 26, 28, 30

# Index